Javelinas

by Conrad J. Storad

Lerner Publications Company • Minneapolis

For Eli, Natalie, and Jacob, my grandchildren. I can't wait to help you explore the wonders of Arizona.

—Grandpa Top

Special thanks to Fran Booth of Booth Communications in Scottsdale, Arizona. Getting to know the javelina herd that lives in the wash near your home was a great help for the completion of this book.

—CJS

The images in this book are used with the permission of: © Joe McDonald/Visuals Unlimited, pp. 4, 28, 33; © Laura Westlund/Independent Picture Service, p. 5; © Tom and Pat Leeson, pp. 6, 36, 39; © Walt Anderson/Visuals Unlimited, p. 7; © Photodisc/Getty Images, p. 8; © Norman Sherman, pp. 9, 15, 17, 26, 34, 47; © Francois Gohier/Photo Researchers, Inc., p. 10; © Phillip Slattery/Visuals Unlimited, p. 11; © Paul & Joyce Berquist/Animals Animals, pp. 12, 20, 37, 42; © Carlos Adolfo Sastoque N./SuperStock, pp. 13, 48 (top); © ZSSD/ SuperStock, pp. 14, 32; © Pete Oxford/Minden Pictures/Getty Images, pp. 16, 41; © Darren Bennett/Animals Animals, p. 18; © age fotostock/SuperStock, p. 19; © Jim Merli/Visuals Unlimited, p. 21; © Craig K. Lorenz/Photo Researchers, Inc., p. 22; © Doug Sokell/Visuals Unlimited, p. 23; © Bayard H. Brattstrom/Visuals Unlimited, p. 24; © James Randklev/ CORBIS, p. 25; © Jeff Foott/Discovery Channel Images/Getty Images, p. 27; © Robert E. Barber/ Alamy, p. 29; © D. Robert & Lorri Franz/CORBIS, p. 30; © SuperStock, Inc./SuperStock, p. 31; © Fran A. Booth, ABC/Booth Communications, Inc., p. 35; © Joe McDonald/Animals Animals, p. 38; © Royalty-Free/CORBIS, p. 40; © Debra Behr/Alamy, p. 43; © Jerry L. Ferrara/ Photo Researchers, Inc., p. 46; © Janine Pestel/Visuals Unlimited, p. 48 (bottom).

Front cover: © Robert Shantz/Alamy.

Lerner Publications Company
A division of Lerner Publishing Group, Inc.
241 First Avenue North
Minneapolis, MN 55401 U.S.A.

Website address: www.lernerbooks.com

Library of Congress Cataloging-in-Publication Data

Storad, Conrad J.
    Javelinas / by Conrad J. Storad.
        p.   cm. — (Early bird nature books)
    Includes index.
    ISBN 978–0–8225–7890–1 (lib. bdg. : alk. paper)
    1. Collared peccary—Juvenile literature. I. Title.
QL737.U59S76 2009
599.63'4—dc22   2007035922

Manufactured in the United States of America
1 2 3 4 5 6 – PA – 14 13 12 11 10 09

Contents

Javelinas live only in North, Central, and South America. The striped areas show where javelinas live.

Be a Word Detective

Can you find these words as you read about the javelina's life? Be a detective and try to figure out what they mean. You can turn to the glossary on page 46 for help.

boar

canine teeth

desert

habitat

herds

hooves

nursing

peccaries

piglings

predators

scent

scent gland

sow

territory

Chapter 1

These are javelinas (HAH-vuh-LEE-nuhz). What kind of animals are javelinas?

Don't Call Me Pig!

You are walking in the desert. You hear noises coming from behind some cactus plants. Ick! Something smells nasty. You stand very still and wait. Then you see a group of animals coming down the trail. What are they?

These animals are javelinas. They look kind of like pigs. They grunt like pigs. But please don't call them pigs. Javelinas and their relatives make up a group of animals called peccaries (PEH-kuh-reez).

Although javelinas look like pigs, they are not pigs.

Peccaries are part of a big group of animals called Artiodactyla (AR-tee-oh-DAK-tuh-luh). Other animals in this group include pigs, deer, antelopes, camels, giraffes, and hippos.

These pronghorn antelopes are related to peccaries.

A javelina has four toes on its front feet. Its back feet have three toes.

All of these animals have hooves. Hooves are feet with hard, tough coverings.

This is a white-lipped peccary. It is bigger than the javelina.
It also has whitish hair on its head.

There are three kinds of peccaries.
Chacoan peccaries live in Mexico. White-
lipped peccaries live in the rain forests of South
America. And javelinas live in the United
States, Mexico, and Central and South America.

Javelinas are also called collared peccaries. This name comes from the ring of gray hair around the javelina's neck. The ring looks like a gray collar.

The scientific name of the collared peccary is Pecari tajacu.
Do you see the gray ring around this javelina's neck?

A javelina weighs up to 60 pounds. That is about as much as a second grader. A javelina has a thin body, skinny legs, small feet, and a short, stubby tail. The tail is hidden beneath the animal's long hair.

A javelina's tail is much shorter than a pig's tail.

A javelina's bristly hair is the color of salt and pepper.

A javelina's hair is thick and bristly. It is black and gray and flecked with white. It looks sort of like salt and pepper mixed together. Javelinas have extra-long hairs along their necks and backs. The hairs are about 6 inches long.

A javelina has two ears, two eyes, and a pink nose.

Javelinas have large heads with flat, wide noses. They have small, round ears and little eyes. Javelinas can't see well. But they have very good hearing. And their sense of smell is excellent.

A javelina has lots of teeth. The teeth in the front of its mouth are small. The teeth in the back of its mouth are large and flat. Four very long, sharp teeth are between the front teeth and the back teeth. The long teeth are called canine (KAY-nine) teeth.

A javelina has 38 teeth in its mouth. Do you see its canine teeth?

Chapter 2

This javelina lives in the rain forest. In what other places do javelinas live?

Spiny, Crunchy Food

A habitat (HAB-uh-tat) is the home area where an animal lives. Javelinas live in many different kinds of habitats. Some javelinas live in hot, dry deserts. Some live in cool forests. And some live in rocky land filled with tough grass and spiny bushes.

This javelina family lives in a desert in the southwestern United States.

This javelina is eating the leaves off a tree.

No matter where javelinas live, they can find food to eat. They are not picky eaters. They munch on all kinds of plants. They eat roots, leaves, flowers, seeds, and fruits. Sometimes javelinas eat parts of dead animals. They may also eat insects or spiders. But javelinas don't kill larger animals for food.

Hungry javelinas can make a big mess. The animals use their tough noses and long canine teeth like shovels. They dig up the ground, looking for plant roots to eat. The animals pull apart yucca (YUH-kuh) and agave (uh-GAH-vee) plants to eat the soft insides. When dinner is over, the ground is covered with torn-up plants.

These are agave plants. Agave is one of the many things that javelinas will eat.

A javelina eats the juicy pad of a prickly pear cactus.

In the United States, most javelinas live in deserts. In the summer, the desert is blazing hot. Water is hard to find. Most soft plants dry up and die. But spiny cactus plants have tough skin. The skin keeps these plants from drying out. They can live through the hot, dry weather. They are full of water that javelinas need to survive a dry summer.

During the summer, desert javelinas search for food in the morning and the evening. These times are cooler than the middle of the day. In the hottest part of the day, javelinas find shady places to rest.

Javelinas rest during the hottest part of the day. These javelinas found a shady spot under a prickly pear cactus.

A javelina can knock over a small barrel cactus. It uses its hooves and sharp teeth to break open the plant. Then it feasts on the plant's soft insides. Javelinas also eat lots of prickly pear cactus pads during the summer.

A javelina nibbles on the fruit of a barrel cactus.

In the fall, seed pods fall off of many kinds of desert plants. Javelinas munch on the seeds of paloverde (PA-loh-VER-day), mesquite (muh-SKEET), and ironwood trees.

Javelinas often eat the seeds of the ironwood tree.

Hungry javelinas also look for pack rat nests. Pack rats are desert animals. They make huge nests out of sticks. They fill the nests with seeds. They save the seeds to eat during the winter. Javelinas dig up pack rat nests. They gobble up all the seeds in one meal.

This is a pack rat nest. Javelinas will search for the seeds that a pack rat has saved in its nest.

This desert in Arizona can get very cool in January.

In the winter, the desert is cooler. The nights are colder than the days. So javelinas search for food during the day. At night, the animals sleep together in a big pile. Snuggling together helps the javelinas to stay warm.

Chapter 3

This is a javelina family. Javelinas live in larger groups too. What are those groups called?

My Family Stinks

 Javelinas live in groups called herds. Each herd has its own territory (TAYR-uh-TOR-ee). The territory is the area of land where the herd lives and looks for food. The territory might cover 1 square mile. That is about the size of a large shopping mall.

The number of javelinas in a herd depends on how much food its territory has. Javelinas that live in places with plenty of food have big herds. If a place doesn't have much food, javelina herds are small. Small herds don't need as much food as big herds. Most herds have 9 to 12 members. Big herds might have 20 or 30 javelinas.

A javelina herd spreads out to look for food.

Javelinas stink. Some people think javelinas smell worse than skunks. But a javelina's stinky smell is very important. It helps the javelina send messages to other javelinas.

A javelina's stinky smell comes from its scent (SENT) gland. The scent gland is a small sack made of skin. It is on a javelina's back, above its tail. The gland is filled with stinky juice called scent.

The javelina's scent gland looks like a small hole above its tail.

This javelina is marking his scent against a tree.

Herds of javelinas use scent to mark their territory. They rub against trees, bushes, and rocks. They squirt stinky scent onto tall objects. The scent is a smelly warning. It means, "This is our herd's territory. Stay out!"

A javelina rubs itself against another member of its herd.

Javelinas also rub their scent on other herd members. The animals' stinky scent mixes together. It makes a special smell for the herd. The smell helps javelinas know who belongs in their herd.

Javelinas sniff other herd members all the time. "Oh, you are my brother." "You are my mom." They sniff rocks and trees too. "Yes, this is our home."

Javelinas sniff each other to make sure they belong together in the herd.

Herd members travel back and forth across their territory. As they walk, they look for plants to eat and water to drink. They also look for safe places to rest.

A herd travels only about 1 mile a day within its territory.

A javelina follows another member of the herd.

The javelinas walk in single file. Their feet step on the same spots. The javelinas' hooves squash grass and other plants. They make trails. The herd uses the same paths again and again.

Chapter 4

Male and female javelinas look alike. What is a female javelina called?

Little Ones

A male javelina is called a boar. A female is called a sow. Baby javelinas are called piglings. Javelinas usually have one baby at a time. But sometimes they have two or even three babies.

Newborn piglings weigh only 1 pound. That's the same as four sticks of butter. The babies are small. But they can stand up and walk the day they are born. The piglings drink their mother's milk. This is called nursing.

These piglings are going to drink their mother's milk.

Each pigling stays close to its mother. It hides under her belly or between her legs. When the javelinas travel, the piglings line up and walk with the herd. If a pigling gets lost, it squeals loudly. The adult javelinas hear the squeals. They run to the baby.

This pigling stays very close to its mother.

This sow and her piglings search for plants to eat.

Piglings grow quickly. When they are 6 weeks old, they start to eat plants. Soon after that, they stop nursing.

Javelinas are fully grown when they are 1 year old. Most javelinas live about 7 years. But some javelinas live to be 15 years old.

Chapter 5

A yawning javelina shows its sharp canine teeth. What do a javelina's teeth have to do with its name?

Teeth Like Spears

There are many stories about how javelinas got their name. One story is about Spanish soldiers. Long ago, these soldiers explored the area that is now the state of Arizona. The soldiers carried long spears called javelins. The soldiers saw herds of peccaries in the desert. The soldiers thought the animals' long, sharp canine teeth looked like spears. So they named the animals javelinas.

Spears are dangerous weapons. Javelinas' canine teeth are dangerous too. Javelinas use their canine teeth to protect themselves and their babies.

A javelina shows its teeth during a fight with another javelina.

Many different predators (PREH-duh-turz) live where javelinas live. Predators are animals that hunt and eat other animals. Coyotes (kye-OH-teez), bobcats, bears, and mountain lions are predators that hunt javelinas. Human hunters kill javelinas too.

Javelinas watch out for one another. If a javelina sees a predator, it barks like a dog. The sound warns the rest of the herd. The javelinas all run in different directions.

This bobcat is a predator of javelinas.

This javelina is on the alert. He is ready to protect the herd.

When danger is near, javelinas clack their teeth together. They growl and show off their canine teeth. They squirt nasty-smelling scent. The long hairs on the javelinas' backs stand up straight. This makes the javelinas look bigger and scarier. The fierce look may scare away a predator. But if the predator stays, the javelinas will fight.

Javelinas use their four long canine teeth to fight. The teeth are very sharp. They can badly hurt a predator. Adult javelinas bite predators to protect their piglings.

Javelina piglings look cute and cuddly. But smart people don't try to pet them or pick them up. The rest of the herd is probably nearby. If the babies squeal, adult javelinas will come running to help them.

This pigling would squeal if you tried to pick it up.

Two javelinas cross a road in a park. The rest of the herd may be nearby.

Javelinas are wild animals. You are lucky if you get a chance to see a herd in the desert. If you do see javelinas, be smart. Watch them from a safe distance. And please, never call them pigs.

ON SHARING A BOOK

When you share a book with a child, you show that reading is important. To get the most out of the experience, read in a comfortable, quiet place. Turn off the television and limit other distractions, such as telephone calls.

Be prepared to start slowly. Take turns reading parts of this book. Stop occasionally and discuss what you're reading. Talk about the photographs. If the child begins to lose interest, stop reading. When you pick up the book again, revisit the parts you have already read.

BE A VOCABULARY DETECTIVE

The word list on page 5 contains words that are important in understanding the topic of this book. Be word detectives and search for the words as you read the book together. Talk about what the words mean and how they are used in the sentence. Do any of these words have more than one meaning? You will find the words defined in a glossary on page 46.

WHAT ABOUT QUESTIONS?

Use questions to make sure the child understands the information in this book. Here are some suggestions:

What did this paragraph tell us? What does this picture show? What do you think we'll learn about next? Where do javelinas live? What is a group of javelinas called? How do javelinas use their stinky scent? How do javelinas make paths in their territories? What are baby javelinas called? What do javelinas do to scare away enemies? What is your favorite part of the book? Why?

If the child has questions, don't hesitate to respond with questions of your own, such as What do *you* think? Why? What is it that you don't know? If the child can't remember certain facts, turn to the index.

INTRODUCING THE INDEX

The index helps readers find information without searching through the whole book. Turn to the index on page 48. Choose an entry such as *babies* and ask the child to use the index to find out what baby javelinas eat. Repeat with as many entries as you like. Ask the child to point out the differences between an index and a glossary. (The index helps readers find information, while the glossary tells readers what words mean.)

JAVELINAS

BOOKS

Dunphy, Madeleine. *Here Is the Southwestern Desert.* Berkeley, CA: Web of Life Children's Books, 2006. Learn about the Sonoran Desert, one of the deserts in which javelinas live.

Johnson, Rebecca L. *A Walk in the Desert.* Minneapolis: Lerner Publications Company, 2001. Find out about other plants and animals that live in North American deserts.

Swan, Erin Pembrey. *Camels and Pigs: What They Have in Common.* New York: Franklin Watts, 1999. This book describes camels, pigs, and other animals that are in the Artiodactyla group with javelinas.

Yule, Lauray. *Javelinas.* Tucson, AZ: Rio Nuevo Publishers, 2004. An authority on the natural history of the Sonoran Desert provides the full story on javelinas.

WEBSITES

Artiodactyls
http://www.enchantedlearning.com/subjects/mammals/classification/Artiodactyls.shtml
This website has links to pages describing javelinas and many other animals in the Artiodactyla group.

The Chacoan Peccary
http://www.hoglezoo.org/animals/view.php?id=210
Learn about the Chacoan peccary, the big cousin of the javelina that lives in hot forests of South America.

DesertUSA
http://www.desertusa.com/life.html
This Web page has information on North America's deserts and the plants and animals that live in them.

GLOSSARY

boar: a male javelina

canine (KAY-nine) teeth: the four long, sharp teeth between a javelina's front teeth and back teeth

desert: a place where little rain falls

habitat (HAB-uh-tat): the home area where an animal lives

herds: groups of javelinas

hooves: feet that have hard, tough coverings

nursing: drinking mother's milk

peccaries (PEH-kuh-reez): piglike animals that live in North America and South America. The javelina is one kind of peccary.

piglings: baby javelinas

predators (PREH-duh-turz): animals that hunt and eat other animals

scent (SENT): a stinky liquid that javelinas' bodies make

scent (SENT) gland: a small sack made of skin above a javelina's tail. The scent gland is filled with stinky liquid.

sow: a female javelina

territory (TAYR-uh-TOR-ee): the area of land where a herd of javelinas lives and looks for food

INDEX

Pages listed in **bold** type refer to photographs.